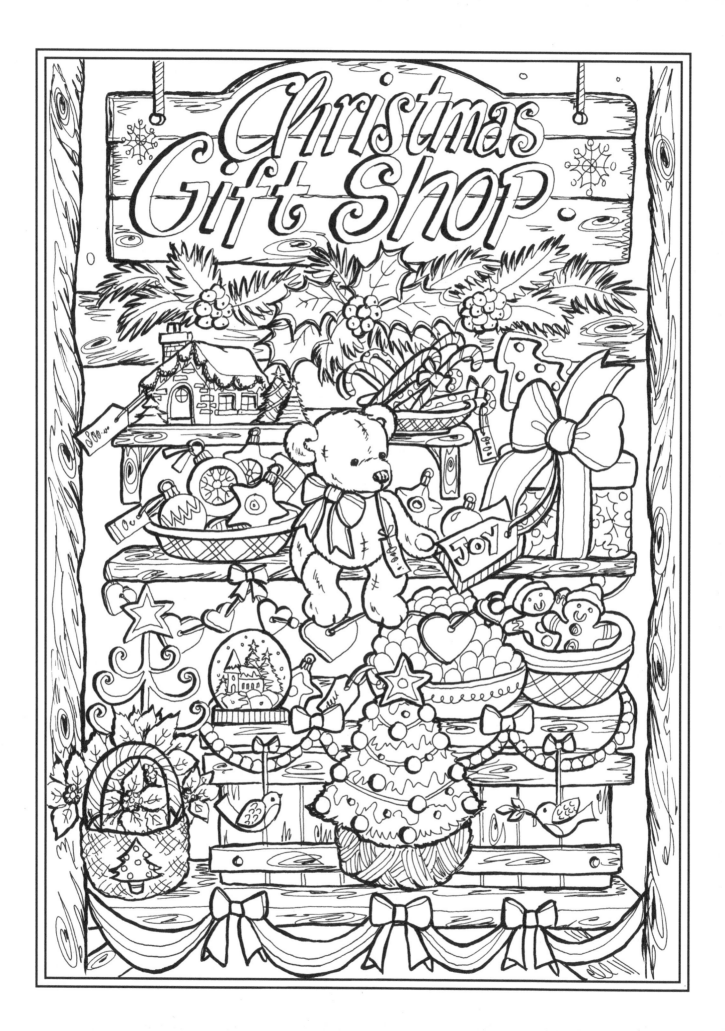

MERRY CHRISTMAS

Inside this beautiful coloring book, you will find the Christmas of your dreams! Set amidst snowy landscapes are quaint houses decorated for the holidays, festive sleigh rides, and children window shopping at a toy store. There are also cozy scenes of fireplaces, Christmas trees, and dogs and cats curled up contentedly. Specially designed for experienced colorists, Creative Haven® coloring books offer an escape to a world of inspiration and artistic fulfillment, and perforated pages printed on one side only make displaying your finished artwork easy.

Copyright

Copyright © 2019 by Dover Publications
All rights reserved.

Bibliographical Note

Country Christmas Coloring Book is a new work, first published
by Dover Publications in 2019.

International Standard Book Number
ISBN-13: 978-0-486-83252-4
ISBN-10: 0-486-83252-X

Manufactured in the United States of America
83252X06   2021
www.doverpublications.com

Country Christmas

COLORING BOOK

TERESA GOODRIDGE

DOVER PUBLICATIONS
GARDEN CITY, NEW YORK